Ghetto Conscious

Evolution of a Rebel

By Brandon Vega

Illustrations David Campbell

ISBN: 978-0-578-65613-7

Illustrations by David Campbell

ATTENTION: SCHOOLS AND BUSINESSES
Brandon Vega is available for select
speaking engagements. To inquire
about a possible appearance, please
contact starteatn@gmail.com or visit
www.starteatn.com. Ghetto Concious
books are also available at quantity
discounts with bulk purchase for
educational, business or sale
promotional use.

In Memory of

Lavel "Pootie Rich" Mucherson

You contributed to who I am today; you may not have lived ideally, but you most certainly steered me the right way. For that you can never be repaid, I've always shown my gratitude, but once again, I'd like to say thanks. Thanks for believing in me. Thanks for looking out for me. Thanks for constantly encouraging me. Thanks for making sure I stayed out of trouble. For all of that, "Main Man..." I love you. Now rest your weary head brother, I know you had been overwhelmed. You fought battles that were beyond this physical realm. So, until we meet again, I pray your soul finds peace. Through all of my work, you will continue to live through me.

New day Soldier! Yay.

"We can easily forgive a child who is afraid of the dark; the real tragedy of life is when men are afraid of the light."

- Plato

This is a testament of faith
As well as a tribute
To all of my ancestors
Humbly working to succeed
The journey is a process
So I remind myself

    Each day

        That I am better...

        Better...

           Than I was yesterday.

Brandon Vega

Contents

In order to understand
The people
You must get to know
The people
Work with
The people
Ingrain yourself in the trenches with
The people
Get your hands dirty with
The people
In order to understand...

The people's struggle

- The People

Introduction

One can be so accustomed to chaos, that when he or she finally arrives into a stable environment, the norm can cause confusion. When the erratic behaviors are no longer deciding factors, they can cause withdrawal and restlessness becoming unbearable to existence. The seduction of believing the intensity of the jungle equates to the survival of being alive, happens in the subconscious mind. It entangles it; leaving the soul longing for a meaningful purpose. The experience of surviving the jungle day in and day out produces heart pounding excitement and fear. One must seek help because (subconsciously) one is addicted to chaos.

On the brighter side, there are pros to growing up in this jungle. The jungle forces one to develop a desperate sense of hunger required to survive the world. A certain kind of mentality. An EATN mentality. EATN is the acronym for Exist Above The Noise. Existing Above The Noise is not allowing self to be discouraged by obstacles or distracted from one's goals during this journey. The jungle replicates the world we live in with all of its noise, distractions and obstacles. Without that focus in the jungle, one's survival may be in jeopardy.

My environment, along with my experiences, shaped me into who I am. Striving to be successful, early in my life I developed a sense of hunger that derived from a desperation to make it. So, I began to search for things to satiate my intellectual hunger. It became imperative that I quench my thirst for knowledge. My ambition innately allowed me to use a gift bestowed upon me. This gift would be basketball. I received a college education during the process. Basketball has been my navigational and motivational tool, which has given me opportunities that have surpassed my imagination.

The purpose of this book is to share the power of resiliency, perseverance and persistence. I want to thank my family, friends and mentors for continuously encouraging me. Most importantly, I would not be who I am if it were not for the environment of Carol City. In the process of maturing I have discovered the environmental exposures and advanced education that have led me to growth and mental acuity. Therefore, I wish to share my experiences as lived to majority, through my poetry.

Ghetto Conscious

The days are long
The nights are cruel
Coming up in the ghetto
Sometimes I wonder
What is a black boy to do?
When he grows up without his daddy
Cause he either dead
Or canned in a cell
How does he not expect
A spot to be reserved
For him in a jail?

Growing up fast
Forced to learn on our own
Difficult when you
Have to teach yourself
The system is flawed
It is designed
For us all to fail
Taking responsibility
You see it starts with me
And nobody else
If I'm going to influence others
I must start with myself

Today things will change
Starting it off
By looking in the mirror
Exhaling as I breathe
Wiping the condensation
To see my reflection
To get a clearer picture
As a black man
I have to be the example
That I want to see
Saving one boy at a time
In our community

We have been down
But never out
Destruction
Only leads to reconstruction
We must get out in the field
Lace up our boots
Put on our hard hats
To make sure
There will be construction
Building boys up in ghettos everywhere
I GUARANTEE
It will be worth it
A new day will soon come
When we are all reformed
Ensuring the Black Male Resurgence

- Black Male Resurgence

13

Ghetto Conscious

Chapter 1
Genesis

Life as I knew it
Before it started
Was about to end
Realizing what life had in store
For a black man
Naturally,
The fear of living
Slowly crept in
Can't tell you
How the story goes
But this is how it begins...

Brandon Vega

Ghetto Conscious

To be quite honest
I'm not sure how I'm even alive
When my grandma conceived my daddy
She was forty-five
Low chance of a safe birth
A miracle my daddy survived
My grandma's only grandson
It was imperative I thrived
My life hung by a thread
There were no guarantees
Why'd God allow grandma to wait so late?
Did he almost forget about me?

I had to be born

        - Born Ready

I was at risk the moment I was born
I figured the least I could do
Was give life a chance
When I was a fetus
I often fantasized about being dead
My birth wasn't natural
My mama had a cesarean
Now that the days were numbered
The clock began

I started thinking outside the box
That had me boxed in
"They" put liquor stores
On every corner
My brain was soaked with...
"Hennessy"
I had known her
Way too prematurely
When my mama was pregnant
She sipped
To decompress
Assuming
She'd improve her memory
Sinking into my amniotic sac
It had gotten into me
Maybe the alcohol
Is what enhanced my creativity

Eventually...
I found my way out

                    - Thinkaholic

Embedded in the concrete jungle
I had to survive
The ferociousness of a young lion
Came from being deprived
Life was moving swiftly
No time to sit around and cry
Everyday I was on the hunt
It was do or die
Difficult avoiding trouble
I can't lie
Knowing better than to question
But God why?

Why would you place me
In an environment like this?
Out of everywhere in the world
You chose the lion's den?
I had no choice but to run with
Tigers, bears and bad men
In the jungle
There was never time
For any friends

I would close my eyes
Open my ears
To closely listen
When the grass was high
I couldn't see
But could hear the hissing
Snakes everywhere
When I spent my money on attention
There were plenty nights
I was saved by
Divine intervention

The fear of failure propelled me
To continue my mission
Want to thank my praying mama
When I didn't believe
And not to mention...
These trials
These tribulations
Are what made me
This is how I rose up
Through the concrete

                    - Rose Up

Brandon Vega

Ghetto Conscious

Chapter 2
Elementary Days

Ghetto Conscious

Early in my life
Elementary school
Is where I excelled
When I was young
Thoughts of the streets
Never occurred
I could never fathom
The possibility of going to jail

When headed in the direction
Of the success way
Being informed of the world
Increase chances to participate
Feeding the mind
Can be a special treat
This is one thing
I can guarantee

- Success

In elementary school
I would answer every question
No matter wrong or right
Wanted my teachers to know
I attempted my homework at night
Insecure with themselves
My peers would tell me
To quit acting white
Never a matter of color
I was just fascinated
With being bright
They thought I was out of my mind
When I appeared in sight
Working to change the narrative
Because the only thing
That comes from darkness
Is light...

That I could not dim for anyone

- Bright

Ms. Lawrence considered me gifted in
the 3rd grade. At the time, I didn't
know what she saw in me. I took school
serious, as well as my grades. I did
all of my work and I was well behaved.
What made me more special than the
other students? Felt I was the same.
Didn't know there was a difference,
until they tried to separate me. To be
amongst the brightest kids would have
been an honor. I never made it to that
gifted class though. It was a while
ago. Let me think back... the day
before I was to transition, I got into
a clash. Aw... what was his name? If I
can recall correctly, it was Donnie.
He picked a fight with me so I had to
put him on his ass. Yeah! Donnie is
the reason I could no longer move to
the gifted class. This really hurt my
feelings. I wasn't a bad kid "per se,"
but I could be a little mischievous.
If I'm remembering right, this would
be the beginning. The beginning of
high anxiety and a conceptual memory
produced toward a negative stimulus.

- The Beginning

Never cared to show
Definitely never one for telling
Supposed to keep it concealed
Whenever you had a weapon
Most of the time I played down
To the competition
In order to develop trust
I had to be deceptive
Compelled to join the line
Growing up I chose to follow
Thought it was imperative if
I wanted to see tomorrow
I believed outsmarting my peers
Would solve this particular conundrum
We didn't play many games
Where I came from
In spite of that,
There was this one particular one...
I did have a favorite game
That I loved to play
I was wise enough to play dumb...

Nobody liked a smart ass

                    - Wizdumb

Some of my friends only came to school
For the free breakfast and lunch
Once school was over
They were back out on the hunt
Had no food at home
Their hands were forced
You see...
If they didn't put in work
Then they wouldn't eat

This would be my introduction
To economic disparities
I was exposed to socioeconomic statuses
Psychosocial stressors were due
To the poverty
Not many opportunities were afforded
Our surroundings had a hold
On positive life qualities
Unfortunately,
This was the sad reality

- Hierarchy

They never drank coffee
But my friends kept a mean mug
Externally kept others away
When internally they needed hugs
Had gangsta personas
They appeared to be dangerous
Maintaining a stale face
Was an absolute must
Them boys would say
"Don't look at me"
Accidental eye contact
Could ignite a fight
Nobody was ever friendly
They wanted others to feel fear
There was no such thing as pity

Always wondered
Why they had to act like that
A lot of problems sparked
From the question...

"Whatchu lookin' at?"

- Mean Mug

When it was time to line up
We lined up alphabetically
Because of my last name
Everyone
Was always ahead of me
Got used to playing the back
Early on my thoughts
Would not allow me to get to the front
After everybody got theirs
All they ever left was crumbs

How could I get ahead?
I had to come up with a plan
Since numbers didn't lie
I had an 80% chance
At failing...
Which left me with
A 20% chance
To succeed
I'm used to coming from behind
Ironic now that I want to lead

- Lineup Strategy

Brandon Vega

My homie couldn't read
Nor could he count
When he weighed money up
Oddly,
He knew the exact amount
All of his life
He had been labeled a crook
Deep down he wanted to do well
Just felt he'd always be overlooked

Together we dove in the books
To comprehend the text
Collecting vital information
To prepare for life's test

Neither one of us
Was exactly computer savvy
Folks barely made ends meet
Couldn't afford Silicon Valley

Where we lived

If you needed something fixed
You could easily find a tech
And if it was really real
Then you needed a vest

Damn near impossible to dodge trouble
Just had to try your best
Every move we made was critical
Life was a game of chess

- Technical Support

Every now and again
I would doze off in class
And I'd wonder...

"IF we valued people
The way we valued things
Then maybe
Just maybe
The world would be a better place..."

•

"Can be here today
And gone tomorrow
Just make sure
You leave something..."

•

"Make sound decisions
Remain silent
When handling business..."

•

"Wisdom. Knowledge. Understanding.
Is all I'll ever ask
With these three ingredients
I can complete any task..."

As the clouds
Hover in the sky
Thoughts
Constantly pass me by
The earth is still
There is not a sound
Taking the time
To look around
It appears there is nothing...

Nothing.
Except my thoughts...

- My Thoughts

I snapped out of the daze
Unfortunately,
I couldn't dwell too long
My only concern now
Was making it home

Brandon Vega

After school dismissals
Were always critical
The majority of my friends
Came to school with pistols
Toward the end of class
I'd give the clock a glance
It was almost time to go...
When the bell would ring
I'd try to be the first to leave
Didn't want to stick around for any
fights
Or the aftermath of Jumanji
At the same time...
I dreaded the long walks home

                    - Dreadful

Ghetto Conscious

Chapter 3
Parting Ways

Upon my arrival home
My parents constantly
Argued back and forth
Everything caved in
As their marriage
Ultimately,
Led to a divorce

Something you mentioned
Bothered me
Heavily
Weighing on my mind
Losing you
Would not be
No fault of mine
Down on myself
Down on us
Thinking about everything
Has made it difficult
To hold my head up

- Hardship

Holding on
For dear life
With the anticipation
Of never letting go
No matter the sacrifices
Despite the splinters
Impaled within my hand
I kept holding on
Down to the very last thread
Yearning for you
As you slowly
Withered away

- Clothespin

Hoping to fix our broken marriage
With a quick repair
Shattered into a million pieces
Feelings everywhere
Mind blown
Heart filled with anguish
And deep despair
To solve our problems
We usually took an elevator
Instead of stairs
Looking for an easy way out
We fell out of love rapidly
The benefits of climbing stairs
Would have improved
Our hearts dramatically
Had we walked at a normal pace

- Challenge

Staring out the window
Hoping you'll show up
Pacing back and forth
Going from couch to window
No signs of you returning
Hope I didn't ruin things
By saying too much...

Some say time heals all
My heart will heal faster
If you answer my calls
Please...
Answer me

I began to drown in tears
Watching our house
Burn to the ground
Why bother calling fire rescue
Not even they
Could stop the blaze
Why waste time saving a house
That was not a home
If neither of us
Were planning to stay

- Arson

All seemed well
During the honeymoon stage
The sun eclipsed
Darkness quickly came
Next we were dealt
Heartache and pain
Diamonds never saved hearts
Love can be
A cut-throat game
Watching you leave
Left me speechless
With no words to say
We were partners
How could you ever
Renege on me?

- Tough Deal

What were my parents thinking?
Making such a selfish decision
Wonder if they ever considered
Me or my sister's feelings...

Probably didn't
During a time like this
Most people only think
Of themselves
Prisoners of the moment
Locked in a cell
On the other hand,
Maybe staying together longer
Than they should have
Was for us
But EVERYTHING goes out the window
When a marriage loses trust

- Collateral Damage

Ghetto Conscious

Chapter 4
Sports Trauma

To keep me distracted from their turmoil
My daddy forced me into playing sports
Guess for me to have an outlet
This could be a positive source
I played football
However,
Basketball became my favorite sport
My game was big
Although I was short
Eventually I would grow
To dominate the courts
But for some odd reason
I didn't receive my mama's support

Brandon Vega

Sports or drugs
Seemed to be the only way out
The neighborhood was riddled with
Drugs and violence
In the jungle
There were limited choices
You could be a ball player
Drug dealer
Or you could go to jail
Worse of them all
You could get gunned down
By shooters
Who got paid for bodies
That recently went on sale
They didn't shoot for scholarships
But for stripes in the streets
Menace to society
So naturally, they disturbed peace
Any night it could be a shootout
Like NBA all-star weekend
Came to visit
The choices we made
Always felt
Like the right decisions

- Pick your poison

I was told early on
That my attitude would be my downfall
Since pee-wee's we were instructed
To kill the man with the ball

At this stage of my life
I am no longer confused
If you the one balling
People might want to hurt you

Seemed because of the hate given
We all were under some type of spell
The jealousy and envy surfaced
Whenever someone excelled

- Killa Man

When we played sandlot football
We played to prevent from clashing
In the streets
I played on teams
With people
That killed people
That played on the same team

Talk about cohesiveness
And camaraderie...

Premeditated murder
Was always encouraged
Trained to kill
Because practice made perfect
At the rate black boys were dying
I thought my life was worthless
Times I felt scared
I learned not to be nervous
Excelled at a young age
Prior to even scratching my surface
Things done involuntarily
Was all for a purpose
Because the constant that remained
Was intellectual alertness

- Practice

When we put on that gear
Instantly,
We became crash dummies
Trying to inflict
As much pain as possible
On one another
I took all my anger out
Because of the lack of support
I received from my mother

- Crash Dummy

Mamas screaming in the crowd
I look up
My mama not around
Mamas rooting
Still searching for my mama
But she's nowhere to be found
If only
My mama would come
To one of my games...
What could she possibly be doing
At this time?
Would she be more supportive
If I lived a life of crime?
Nope she wouldn't
It would serve me best
If she was in the crowd
Cheering and rooting
She wanted me to stay out of trouble
And away from the streets
That is the only reason
I stayed on the basketball team

I've dealt with pain
I've been enraged
I've been on the outside looking
At times I've gone insane
All because my mama
Didn't show up to my games

- Child Support

On the other hand,

My daddy always showed up
But it felt like
My good was never good enough
Instead of acknowledging
That he was proud
After basketball tournaments
He would say
"For this type of performance
I'd be damned
If I'm gone keep driving out of town
You need to score more
Stop passing like you Magic
Take your man off the dribble
And get to the basket"

I guess early on
I knew life was a team game
Watching someone else score
When I assisted
To me was all the same

- Helping Hand

Words are powerful. Did my daddy
say things to light a fire under
me? Hmmm... not quite sure... but
maybe. During this time, I couldn't
understand it; just letting it be
known that it caused emotional damage.
Most times I questioned myself. I was
very indecisive, my confidence dipped.
The criticism was way too critical.
If I didn't perform up to a certain
level, on the way home, I would get
ridiculed. All I ever knew was I never
wanted to be "duck soup." If you were
considered duck soup, then it meant
you were not good in your respective
sport. This would be my motivation to
get busy on the court.

At least, I had my daddy around;
because most of my friends didn't.
The absence of their daddies caused
them to be rebellious. I just rolled
with the punches and decided to accept
it. Although I felt at times my daddy
was being selfish. Did he ever try
to vicariously live through me? Or
was he expecting more than I expected
of myself, because he saw greatness
within me?

- At Least

Chapter 5
se to House

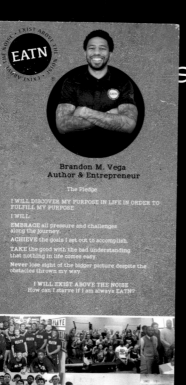

Brandon M. Vega
Author & Entrepreneur

The Pledge

I WILL DISCOVER MY PURPOSE IN LIFE IN ORDER TO
FULFILL MY PURPOSE

I WILL:

EMBRACE all pressure and challenges
along the journey.

ACHIEVE the goals I set out to accomplish.

TAKE the good with the bad understanding
that nothing in life comes easy.

Never lose sight of the bigger picture despite the
obstacles thrown my way.

I WILL EXIST ABOVE THE NOISE
How can I starve if I am always EATN?

Stay Connected:

starteatn@gmail.com
email

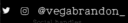 **@vegabrandon_**
Social handles

www.starteatn.com
Website

Ghetto Conscious

After my parents divorced
I fell into a dark space
Started to become more observant
Of everything that went on around me
There was a paradigm shift
That suddenly occurred
My mama would send me off
Whenever I got on her nerves

Tired of being broke
This ain't right
To keep em' on
We have to keep off the lights
Lighting candles when it's dark
To preserve electricity
A sauna in the crib
Talk about heat
It is what it is
Can't afford to fix the A.C.
Besides I don't get paid
Till next week
The way the bills roll in
Have me worried to death
Before I even see it
Uncle Sam dig in my check
Landlord come by everyday
I ain't paid him yet
Bill collectors keep calling
Looking for theirs
I owe Grandma some money
We can't go round there
Poor budgeting
Poor money managing skills
Can't live comfortably
Cause' all the money for bills
Said mama

- Broke

Once told my mama
I hated her
Because she didn't buy me
A pair of shoes
Vividly remember it happening
As she was dropping me off to school
Didn't realize the money
To get what I wanted
Was for the bills and food
Infuriated since I didn't understand
My head began to fume...
I thought...
This woman doesn't support me
This is the least she could do
Reflecting on my younger days
Boy was I confused...
Earlier in my life
It felt as if
I didn't get along with my mama
For no reason at all
I always gave her problems
Maybe these things occurred
Due to my subconscious
Now all I can say is
I'm sorry mama...

- Sorry Mama

I would go to my cousins' house
for the weekend. My cousins are
practically brothers. When we got
together it usually meant trouble. I
had my own bed at home and never had
to fight for any meals. But when I
got around their house; it was about
survival, so for food I would kill.
It was every man for himself when
it came to the kitchen. For the last
cup of Kool-Aid, I would be hoping
and wishing... that there was some
left. All of my cousins were bigger
than me. When we got into it, I would
get my ass beat. The resilience was
cultivated due to having to fight for
everything. A spot to play the game,
spot in line for dinner, spot in line
to take a bath, I even had to fight
for a spot in bed. If I was lucky,
I'd get to sleep with covers. Being
at their house definitely made me
tougher.

- The Green House

If anybody was looking for me
They could find me over there
As much as I was there
My address should've been
The same as theirs
Tony, Nick and Jr
Are my brothers
Their mama is my mama
That remains true to this day
After Lisa Frazier
My heart goes out
To Maria Lawrence aka "Betty"
That lady taught me a lot
And she always kept it real
The things my mama wouldn't discuss
Betty always revealed

- Family

Across the street from my cousins'
house there was a man named Mr.
Charles. He was like the neighborhood
daddy. I admired him for all he did.
He sacrificed personal time to spend
time with kids that were not his. Mr.
Charles was my first basketball coach.
I would be in his backyard all the
time playing and working on my game.
Mr. Charles was not an ordinary man.
When we had games on Saturdays, he
would pack everyone up in his van.
After games, he would feed everyone
on our team. His acts of kindness
and willingness to do things when he
didn't have to, was something I always
paid close attention to. The epitome
of what a role-model should be, he
exemplified it with actions rather
than talk. Mr. Charles was a man of
few words anyway.

- Mr. Charles

When I was at my daddy house
I remember calling him
All the time
To ask if he'd bring home
Something to eat
He would ask
"Is there food in the frigerator?"
I'd reply "Yeah"
Then he'd say
"Nigga you ain't hungry..."

"If you was you'd eat whatever's in there
I ain't spending no money
You better get yo ass in there
And make you a sandwich or sumn'"
Why can't he bring back something?
I got tired of eating sandwiches
And leftover food
He could bring something back
On his way home from school

This was another lesson
If you were hungry you would eat
At the same time,
He would get mad
If the frigerator was left empty

- You ain't hungry

Damn if I did
Be damned if I didn't
When I did eat
I'd get cursed out
For constantly being in the kitchen

My daddy would always say
"You don't have a job
The way you eat is ridiculous
You'll see when you get older
Groceries are expensive"

"And you better not eat my Oreos"
When he opened the pack
He counted the cookies in each row
If there was one missing
My daddy would know

My daddy never made any promises
He never said yes or no
I was given a parking lot speech
Before we entered any stoe'

He would say

"Don't look at nothing
And don't ask for anything"
Instead of saying yes or no
He'd always say "we'll see"

When he did say yes
He most certainly kept his word
But my daddy saying "yes"
Was something I seldomly heard

- We'll See

There's a saying

"It takes a village to raise a kid"

When I wasn't being watched over
That's what my neighborhood did...

Chapter 6
The Neighborhood

Ghetto Conscious

My geographic
Was commonly tragic
No matter what you prayed
Or wished for
There was no voilà
Was no such thing as magic
When you wanted things done
You had to take action
If the jungle didn't kill you
Then you had to worry about
The poachers attacking
Times were difficult
Measures appeared drastic
Never a stroll in the park
At any moment
It could've gotten Jurassic

Ghetto Conscious

Crime infested neighborhood
Is why the cops always raid
My friends were easily bugged
That's why they were quick to spray
And although we couldn't afford them
We understood we were playing for big stakes
I never anticipated getting shot
Yet, I wouldn't hesitate to vaccinate

- Hood Immunity

Brandon Vega

As bad as I wanted to wear a chain
I did not want
To put a noose round my neck
The people in my neighborhood
Would hang me for it
Just so they could wear it themselves

- Hangman

Ghetto Conscious

You wanted your chain to be seen
There was no point
In wearing jewelry tucked
You'd risk the possibility
Of being robbed
Eventually giving your jewelry up
If you weren't out with your family
It was best you left your jewelry home
Gold is more valuable than silver
Still, nothing outweighed the chrome

Brandon Vega

Sirens wailing loud
Cops racing to the scene
Yellow tape all around
Drawing large crowds
Never surprised
Just wondering...
"Who's been murdered now?"
News anchors
And cameras are set
Looking for a story
Little do they know
The killer...
Lives next door to me

                    - Next Door Neighbor

Crimes occurred frequently
Most killings never made the news
There was only one lineup
I wanted to be a part of
And it wasn't the one
Someone could point you out
To pick or choose...
A lot of times
Accused for crimes
We didn't even do
If I was going to be exempt
From getting caught up
God was going to have to be
My refuge

The world does enough judging
Why would I want
A judge judging me?
Had to distance myself
From certain friends
To the block I became an absentee
Didn't want to get lost in the cracks
My whole life I desperately tried
To squeeze my way through
If people thought
You had a chance to win
They'd want you to lose
Fortunately, for me
I was given a chance
Some of my friends
Didn't get the same breakthroughs
If you were stuck in the same place
Your whole life
I'm pretty sure
It could possibly break you

- Fortunate

Pulling ourselves
Out of situations
Was as difficult
As pulling from the rock
King Arthur's sword
Before we knew our worth
Brandishing hammers
Was so common
We didn't have to be Thor

- Worthy

My neighborhood was filled with
Quick Draw McGraws
Everybody in my neighborhood
Was an artist
They loved to draw...
Searching for ends
But didn't quite know
Where to start
The art of hustle...
The art of war...
Maybe it was
The art of simply being bored
Intrigued by the streets
Eager to jump off the porch
Some of my friends lived by it
So *consequently*
They died by the sword

- War of Art

Chilling in the neighborhood
Becoming unprogressive
When cars passed
Everyone became superstitious
Whenever they smoked or drank
They became intemperate
Hurt people
Hurt people
Murder was the only way
Some of my friends
Knew how to handle conflict...

Conflict resolution
Hadn't been taught
In our institution
The way we learned to solve problems
Was by scrapping it out
Or by shootin'
Conflict seemed inevitable
Pain was deeply rooted
Engaging in war
Looking for fights
We were such opportunists
When soldiers died
Kids were quickly recruited
After the dust cleared
Property values dipped
Leaving our neighborhood secluded
The illusion of separateness worked
Preventing us from finding our beginning
And "they" knew this
We couldn't see a way out
The environment made us ruthless

- Noble Truth

Ghetto Conscious

Whether you wanted to
Or not
You could easily get enrolled
Friends were going away early
After 10 or 20 years
We hoped
They'd get paroled

Without going through orientation
Neighborhood involvement
Consisted of guilt by association
Enemies would never pardon us
For good behavior
Your survival depended upon
How you handled certain situations

There were times I felt
I wasn't going to make it
Far as my experiences went
Getting out was as difficult as
Decoding The Matrix
While my friends were hustling
Basketball was going to be my ticket

I just had to remain patient

- Ticket Out

We had no door bell
That never kept the
Shots from ringing
House phone stayed off the hook
Still shots kept ringing
There was no choir to harmonize
That never kept the guns from singing
Listening to bullets ricochet
Off car windows
Would eventually...

Become music to my ears
Like listening to
Beethoven's 9th Symphony
In crescendo
I saw a lot walking back and forth
To that green stoe'
From drunks to prostitutes
Down to drugs being sold
At this point of my life
I wonder...
If I would've died young
How would my story have been told?

Ghetto Conscious

Chapter 7
Crossroads

I had a difficult time
Trying to navigate
My behavior
Was becoming inappropriate
Things just started happening
I became somebody I wasn't
So my friends wouldn't clown me
Trying to be down
Almost drowned me

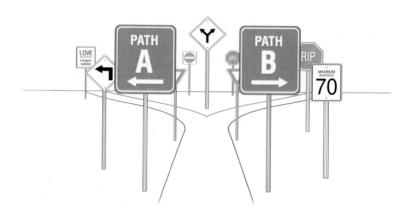

Going nowhere fast
Then life catches up
As adolescents
Why are we in such a rush?
My GPS malfunctioned
Self deception
Led me down a road
I didn't want to travel
Pretending to be someone else
The projection I portrayed
Was completely false
Early on I allowed my environment
To dictate my personality
All because I didn't want
My friends to make fun of me

- Self Deception

In this dark loveless world
It's dark everywhere I go
People are filled
With so much hate
It's dark everywhere I go
The world is consumed with
So much negativity
It's dark everywhere I go
Feels like I can't get away
I keep my eyes closed
To try an escape
But there's this dark cloud
That continues
To linger over me

- Darkness

Going wherever the wind takes me
Getting lost out at sea
I must find self
Before others can find me
As the ship sails out
Dark clouds arise
A storm is coming
There is no surprise
The wind is blowing
The sea is choppin'
Twisting and turning
Steadily rocking
The ocean is having her way
Showing it is no match
Decided to set sail
Now there is no turning back...

- No turning back

Brandon Vega

Swimming in thought to find you
The water engulfed my memory
Drowning as the anchor
Pulled me deep below the sea
Sinking further from the light
Darkness emerged when I saw your face
Reaching for you
I thought...
You could be saved
At arm's length to grab you
Pressure began to pick up
Then all of a sudden
I had been crushed

- Lifeguard

Coming from a long line
Of Stolen Greatness
They got us boxed in the ghetto
Pipelines leading straight to cages
Has to be better seats in this house
All "y'all" got is this section 8 shit?
System has been detrimental
Thinking "y'all" helping but "y'all" really taking
Fathers out of households
Make no mistake and...

The system was put in place
To ensure "y'all" self preservation
Independent from us
So "y'all" formed a declaration
To keep us down down
With all that coded language
And from now on its Juneteenth
The 4th we no longer celebrating...
By the way
Can we get a decent education?
What these schools teaching
Won't help us reach our final
destination

- Stolen Greatness

Some of my friends
Barely knew their A-B-C's
This was problematic
Based on their family history
All they ever knew
Was avoid the F-E-D's
The alphabet boys were inevitable
Their report cards
Were full of F's and D's
When it came to effort
All they got was 3's
No one was concerned
With their education
As a result,
They did poor academically
This had an affect on me
I was always told
You are the company you keep
Once an 'A' and 'B' student
All of a sudden
My grade's began to slip to C's
Then to D's
When I received my first F
I lied about getting my report card
So my daddy wouldn't see
Following friends
Led me in this direction
Being considered dumb
Was so embarrassing

- Poor Grades

Way before any Kodak moments
Project babies was all I hung around
They knew how to have fun
All my friends were classroom clowns
Taking part in their circus
To hide what was on the surface
Couldn't let anybody see
That deep down I was hurting
Tried soul searching
But a cast was on my soul
Holding on to all of my feelings
Unable to express verbally
What I felt
Erupting inside
Bound to blow
My spirit had been crushed
I didn't want to walk in my own shoes
This would become a good reason
To avoid school

- Big Skipper

I remember a teacher telling me
"The way you behave
Makes it hard to see
How you will live to be 18"
Because I was ignorant
I started chuckling
In all actuality
I'm glad I was naïve...
Her words could've come to fruition
If I didn't change my ways
Self-destruction
Could've possibly led
To an early grave
The bed I was making
I didn't even want to lay in
I played due to my immaturity
Without realizing the difference
Between a pencil and a pen

We use to play tag
Till the cops said
"FREEZE"
Member the time
Me, Nick and Chaz
Fit the description
Of an armed robbery
Just sitting in a car
Then came the police
Next thing that ensued
Was the brutality
Snatched out the car
Guns pointed to our heads
"Don't fucking move or your ass is dead"
Five-minutes prior
We were laughing and playing
Never in a million years did we think
We'd end up in this circumstance
The only thing that saved us
Was Mr. Charles Correction Officer's
jacket
When the police asked who it belonged to
Chaz said "It's my daddy's"

- Wrong Place Wrong Time

Shadow boxing demons
That I could not see
When I swung it sounded as if
Someone laughed hysterically
This was a dream
Generated from nightmares
Held this pain for so long
These were feelings I could no longer bear
Afraid to talk to anyone
Didn't think nobody would care
Harbored all my emotions
Because in our communities
Feelings were not to be shared...

I didn't want anyone to think I was soft

- Harbored Emotions

I began to jot down my feelings
Couldn't think of any other way
To freely express myself
So I decided to reach
For the journal up on the shelf
From this night forward
I would submit my deepest thoughts
Writing gave me a sense of hope
When I felt all was lost

- Submit

You the only one that will protect me
You the only one that won't neglect me
You the only one I can tell everything to
When my day is hard I can talk to you
You the only one that I can trust
You the only one I can give my word
You the only one I can complain to
Without feeling like
I'm getting on your nerves
You the only one that listens
You the only one that know all my feelings
You the only one that know all my business
To all of my secrets you are a witness
You the only one that gives me my space
You the only one I don't have to chase
You the only one that gives me all of
your time
Journal you will never be replaced

                    - Confidant

Ghetto Conscious

Chapter 8
Internal Compass

Ghetto Conscious

I would sit and listen
To gangsta's trade war stories
Exchanging admiration for those
Who obtained street glory
Reminiscing with friends
Although the details were gory
I would soon find out
That the streets weren't for me

Brandon Vega

Ghetto Conscious

If you pointed a gun
You most certainly
Had to put it to use
I would turn down open shots
But when contested
I would never hesitate to shoot
Wanted to be a killer
So I picked up a basketball
Options were limited
It was shoot shots
Or shoot my shot
Sell rocks
Or push the rock
Work the trap
Or break traps dribbling
My neighborhood promoted violence!
Therefore,
I would kill.
Or die.
For a scholarship.

- Do or Die

My motor was high; I was ultra
competitive. I was a sore loser
and I didn't take coaching well. I
deliberately went against the grain.
Coach Rob told me I was the future
of Carol City when I was in the 7th
grade. He handed me the keys before I
knew what was expected of me. Feeling
myself, I thought I was above everyone
else. Then Coach Rob burst my bubble
by placing my talents on the shelf.
He'd always say "No one man is bigger
than the program." My childishness
allowed me to think... "shhhit, I am."
Coach Rob would also say "There is no
"I" in team." I knew that, but there
was a "ME." This attitude ultimately
got me kicked off the team. Since
I had nothing else to do, I was no
longer interested in playing college
hoops. Another key lesson, when
you go against the coaches you will
always lose. Coach Rob was teaching
me a lesson at the time that I didn't
comprehend. He was trying to teach me
about life, as well as being a man.

- Team Sport

When I got kicked
Off of the basketball team
All roads were leading
Toward the streets
When I was on the court
Felt I had indescribable abilities
Through the game of basketball
I figured God
Would grant me the serenity
To help alleviate the pain
Of my reality
Because the game
Always took my mind off my problems

- Artistry

Standing on the block
Feeling like a goner
Home feels so far away
Although it's just around the corner
Got two choices
While standing out here dealing
Either I'm gone end up a homicide
Or I'm gone end up killing
Leading straight to an early grave
Or in somebody's prison

- Multiple Choice

Hustled for presidents
Figured having them behind me
Would push for my election
In the streets
Only thing the political gain caused
Was envy and jealousy
Only wanted the money
Never sought any beef
Nor did I want the attention
Now everybody looking for me
"Get out the game"
Said my intuition...
I was just trying to maneuver
The hustler way
To get into the right position

- Dead Presidents

A gun was pointed at me
I didn't know what to think
Just thought to myself
Life could be over in a blink
Staring down the barrel
I became anxious
Go ahead...
Shoot I thought
We'll just become statistics
Subtracting two lives
Adding to these
Black on black killings
Do something different
Don't let the environment
Dictate who you are
There is a chance at redemption
You may be angry
At your circumstances
But you don't
Have to be vindictive

- Redemption

Told my homie
"Don't do it
Don't throw your life away man
If you erase him
You definitely going to the pen
You got better things to do
What you killing for anyway?
Whatever the reason
Won't suffice
For you to spend life
In a cage"

- Think about it

Brandon Vega

My soul was burning
Clutching on my burner
Hallucinating from the drugs
On my mind was murder
The sky was dark as the abyss
The night was cold
Swore on my dead brother
That I would stick to the code
Gone get them niggas
That shot my brother
Anybody can get it
Even they mother
Out for blood I'm locked in
Only seeing red
It's on sight
I swear these niggas is dead

Then it began...

"Don't do it"
Said a little voice
On my shoulder
But the devil telling me
To go through with it
Caught between right and wrong
Devil said "fuck that
Your brother is gone"
The little voice said
"It won't comfort you
You'll still be all alone"
Weighing my options
Since I was no longer stoned
Thought to myself...
God will handle it
And I took my ass home

                - Let God

Once took an oath
Vowing to never cooperate with police
Frowned upon to be a rat
But encouraged to get cheese
What I look like killing a nigga
Leaving him for dead in the street?
Even when it was warranted
I shied away from the beef...
It took a great deal to refrain from
Killing was never me
Although an eye for an eye
Was something I always believed
If I lived this way
God wouldn't be pleased...
How could I hurt my brother
If I know he is blind?
I'm going to give you a pass
And disregard this time
I'm not going to kill you
Cause you hurt my pride

Ohhh no...

                    - Oath

Lifted up
To get out of character
My motor started to flutter
No longer could I crank up
To commit a horrific accident
Restricted by the missing strap
Retracting my seat as I cooled down
I'm glad a big mistake was not made

- Transformer

I would hear em' calling my name
Everyone was shooting
Except for me
We all had goals
We all had dreams
If you aren't shooting for the stars
Redirect your aim
No one wants a piece of your struggle
But will gladly
Take a slice of your fame
A diamond in the rough
It would be a damn shame
If I don't make it out
Will my environment
Accept the responsibility?
Will it take the blame?

- Diamond in The Rough

Ghetto Conscious

Chapter 9
Rich

My big homie was a drug dealer
To his defense
It's all he ever knew
But when it came to me
Getting an education
He always encouraged school
He would always say
"Even though I live wrong
I don't want this for you
That's why I got you under my wing
Giving you game
Blessing you
With these jewels"

The only place
Success came before work
Was in the dictionary
We knew death was real
When we saw
Our friends' pictures in obituaries
Tried making fast money
But it only stuck around temporarily
Even though what we did was wrong
Our motive was forever financial
security
Seen as a sign of weakness
If one sought out therapy
The burden of being black alone
Can cause P.T.S.D.
Murder, Violence, Abuse
All things we grow accustomed to
Living fast and dying young
In the ghetto
Felt like the only dream
That would ever come true

- Help

My heart began to shrink
When I was inducted into the streets
The Hall of Fame ceremony
Only comes when you're deceased
Staring at the roof of the church
As the pastor preach
The out of body experience
Of watching my mama weep
Crying on the floor
Dropping to her knees
That gave me chills
It did something to my soul
Leaving an affect on me
Told myself get out the game
The world has more to offer
"If" I adjust the way I think

- I Want Out

Vio-lence
Got played like violins
Sharks out of water
The sight of blood
Made them grin
Justifying means
By way of sin
Too many losses
Will make one
Desperate for a win...
Have morals
Have values
Don't disregard another life
Before you commit that crime
Be sure to think twice

When Jack got out of the box
He changed the way he thought
He was trapped for so long
His spirit was almost lost
Something got to him
Before he was completely ruined
Turned his life over
And allowed God to work through him
After his stint
He chose to repent
The life he lived
Was in his rear view
It was time to show the world
His resilience and strength

- Jack in The Box

Rich had these famous sayings...

Every time Rich spoke I listened.

He always had something interesting to say.

"Stay sharp
Stay on your toes
PAY attention
Attention is the only thing
You don't lose money paying for
Essentially it is free!"

●

"Even if your pocket's empty
And you dead broke
You can still
Enrich people's lives
It don't cost nothing
To be a decent person"

●

"Fitting in
Will get you axed out
Don't pretend
To be someone
That's not you
You have a gift
You gone waste
Cause'
'You want to be cool'"

"The future belongs to those
Who have vision
I mean those that can truly see
Things past the horizon
That hasn't even risen
Don't be tempted
By the first thing
That peaks your interest
Take a moment to evaluate
So you can make
Good decisions"

•

"Positive thoughts
Determine outcomes
Focus and determination
Generate the income
Pray for it
Dedicate yourself to it
Then hustle for it
That's a Mill Plan"

Racing to beat time
As the time stands still
Numbers are man made
Therefore,
Time is not real
Day is represented by sun
Night is represented by moon
If you arrive early
Does it mean you've arrived too soon?
What if you're late?
What exactly does that indicate?
Would you've arrived early
If you were interested in the place?
Back to the race
Which is short lived
Your time on earth is valuable
Please don't rush it

Ghetto Conscious

Learn to pace yourself
Life's a marathon not a sprint
Remember...
The tortoise challenged the hare
Because he knew he'd win
Don't compare your life
To social media
Never measure yourself up to friends
We'll see who last
When we see who's standing in the end
Don't worry about popularity
Or the latest trends
It's about being the last
Of the Mohicans

- Pace

Don't get down on yourself
When it seems like
Everyone else is winning
Remember in baseball
There are 9 innings
Being down in the beginning
Doesn't mean you're finished
You can get back in the game
If you stay focused
And handle your business
Focus on getting on base
Instead of hitting home runs
Take your time
The game was never won
In inning one

- Long Game

Rich never encouraged me to do wrong
He was a positive influence
He always gave me game
Whenever I was under his tutelage
Didn't really make sense
Because the way he lived
Wasn't quite congruent
Seemed like he had a plan
For my life
That he didn't want me to ruin
If I was doing wrong
He'd let me know
He wasn't cool with it
Each day was a lesson
He was always tutoring
One day he said
"Stay on the path
The streets not where you want to be
If I catch you out here messing round
You gone have to deal with me"

- Tutor

Chapter 10
Puppy Love

Love is mental
Love is gentle
Love is kind
Love is divine
Love is compatibility
Love is chemistry
Love is emotion
Love is devotion
Love is open
Love is potent
Love is trust
Love is tough
No one said love was easy
But...
Love is Love.

I met this girl named Alicia
That was so in love with me
She was my little boo
You know how that puppy love be
The day we met
I didn't want it to end
Before the clock struck midnight
I asked God for eternity...

- Cinderella

Stargazing through my telescope
Noticing one particular star
No need to look around girl
You know who you are
Since you've been discovered
There has never been
A better blessing in disguise
My attention is forever paid
To the heavens in the sky

- Indebted

As our Ferris wheel turns
Wonder where we'd end up
Pray we'd reach the top
Then our ride gets stuck
Malfunctioning
At its highest point

- Highest Point

Afraid of everything
Until you came in my life
Used to live in the dark
Then here came your light
Comforting me
Assuring everything would be alright
Now I'd rather skip through the day
And hop straight into the night
You gave me the courage to love
With all of my might
Trusting you with my heart
Allowing fear
To drift away like a kite

- Happiness

When I look into your eyes
Becoming mesmerized as I gaze
When I listen to you speak
The world goes mute
When I smell your scent
I mistake your name for Rose
When I'm with you
I feel as if
I've arrived in heaven
When I think of you
I become exultant

More than grateful
For the time we've spent
The joy you give
You're more than a blessing
I thank God everyday
That we're more than friends
An asset to my life
You're heaven sent

- Woman of My Dreams

Strolling through the park
A tree whispers to me
"Make sure you come back
I don't like to see you leave"
All the others have left
So why can't I?
She responded
"If you leave
I'll break down and cry
The others always change up
During this time of year
To no surprise...
Lying as they've grown on me
Saying they'll always be here
I want you to remain
Out of them all
Our bond is much deeper
Please don't fall..."

Off

- Fall

Chapter 11
Heartbreaker

The first time I met love
I really fell for her
Then as time went on
The side effect began to affect me
Like a drug
Started to wear me down
Instead of holding me up
As the pressure turned on
I no longer wanted the love
Finding plenty of excuses
I just couldn't commit
After a short period of time
Our relationship would end

You looked past my deficiencies
Choosing to see the best in me
Instead of giving up
You'd rather argue, kick and scream
Our time dwindled away
In the end you were completely over me
I'm sure you were tired of all
The emotional suffering

- Tired

Wasting everything on me
Except your time
Walking all over me
As if I weren't present
How can or why should I accept this?
Laid out flat
My arms and legs are spread
Added to your life for decorations
To show others you have me
That you own me
Tired of you stepping all over me
I am worthy of better
So I'm dusting myself off
This really sucks
No longer will I allow you
To treat me like your rug

Did everything in my power
For you to accept me
Tangled with my emotions
Now my heart keeps rejecting
You've shown me all along
I just refused to see the message
Wondering if you ever loved me
But I already know the answer
To my question

- Rejection

I gave you my heart
You played with the key
Fooling around with it
It was sure to get lost
My body was yours to have
You weren't responsible enough
You never loved me

- Loose Key

When it came to girls
My parents never gave me
The talk about
"The *birds* and the *bees*"
The only thing
I ever got was...

"You bet not bring home no babies."

Alicia, when I got you pregnant
I ignored all of your feelings
I was more concerned with what
I was going to hear from my parents
Worst of all, when you got the abortion
I didn't go to show any support
I was a coward, despite it all
You still wanted us to work
These memories are difficult
To continuously stomach
You were trying to tie me down
But from love, I kept on running
I don't ever expect to rekindle an old
flame
Our time together caused you so much pain
I'm stepping up now
And I'm accepting the blame
Our relationship was ruined
Because I chose to play games
Now that I'm older
I'm confronting these demons
Sorry for all of the hurt I caused
I really mean it
Not one to dwell on the past
But I'd rather not live with regret
These feelings I've ignored for so long
Have made me sick
You was trying to get a boy to be a man
Truth be told, I just wasn't ready yet

Catching bodies
Accepting all kinds of spirits
Messing with me mentality
They got me all twisted
Thought it was love
But it was only lust
All these girls just
Been getting me caught up
Mechanics of my roof
Suddenly contaminated
Wouldn't be thinking this way
If everything was laminated
Protect self at all cost
If you know you can't afford no baby
Try not to jump in the game too soon
Sit back and watch
Be sure to learn the rules
Understand what you're getting yourself into
Sex is much more
Than physical

-Much More

Chapter 12
Lucid Dreams

Ghetto Conscious

Never enjoyed turnovers
It was time to pick up the ball
Before the alarm clock went off
I had been receiving wake up calls
I was living a false reality
That I needed to cease
Then all of a sudden
I started having
These unexplainable dreams

Ghetto Conscious

My mind has walked away
Plenty of times
Often it goes astray
At times I felt it was lost
In which it would never return
Whenever it decided to come back
It would pack up to leave again
This time I gave it a curfew
Asking if it would be back by ten

I had some things to think about...

    - Mind Wanders

Brandon Vega

An eternal sleep might be peaceful
Nobody'll bother me

But...

What if I don't make it to heaven?
Do I deserve a happy eternity?

Foolishly dreaming...
Thinking I'd never get out of here
Its been a hell hole
Such a terrible nightmare
My friends have died
Still I'm searching for answers
Although tough times are inevitable
I must keep my head up
Despite the hardships
The sun started to follow me
If I kept rowing my boat
My life would become a dream

- Sunshine

Each time I've fallen
I've gotten back up
In the process of
Brushing myself off
In my mind
I thought...

Only I could help me
One day I fell so hard
The pain was excruciating
I could feel death tugging
This time
I didn't have the strength
To rise to my feet
When my intercessory cry
Reached the skies
Heaven had drawn back
Open came its curtains
A hand reached down
And a voice from the heavens
Said softly "Be strong and courageous
I am always with you
I promised you would not be forsaken"

- Deuteronomy 31:6

My physical frame was escorted
My mind roamed freely
I watched an eagle soaring
As I gazed from atop the prairie
He glid around for awhile
Until he landed on my shoulder
Strangers prior to our encounter
But for some odd reason I felt like
I already knew him
He whispered
"We are strong enough to walk on air"
I wasn't spiritually in tuned
So I didn't catch a glimpse of the stairs
Our encounter was deeper
Then I initially realized
Could this have been a blessing
In disguise?

- What A Dream

Where could I gain my crown?

Was heaven merely another ghetto?

Brandon Vega

After the edible was digested
I laid down round eleven
Must have dozed off
Strangely,
I found myself in heaven
Looking around confused
To my surprise
I was at a bar-b-que
Observing my surroundings
I heard a familiar voice
"I'm just trying to chill
I don't mean to be rude
Trying to enjoy the festivities
I ain't trying to do no interview"
It was Pac

Then I saw Huey P. Newton
Politicking with a couple of brothers
One of the them was Fred Hampton
I overheard him say
"Boy had them pigs not bombarded
It was gone be on and cracking
I was just getting started...
I've let bygones be bygones
I'm no longer cold hearted
Boy I'm really glad we in heaven
God sure knows how
To throw a good party

Over by the grill
It was Marcus Garvey and Bob Marley
Having open dialogue
Discussing the origins of Rastafari
The ladies laughed at all of the men
They were elated to be together
Maya Angelou beamed her smile
That could persuade any cloudy weather
Then Ms. Tubman emerged
From the massive crowd
Demanding and bossing
All the men around
Billie Holiday placed her arm around her
Reminding her they were in heaven now
Rosa Parks stood up to complain
That it was too much sitting down
At her request
Jam Master Jay cut the music up loud

Trumpets started playing
It was Satchmo and the band
Malcolm and Rosa
Took each other by the hand
Taking it back to Harlem
With that ol' swing dance
Boy they were playing
Such a fine tune
My foot tapped involuntarily
Naturally, I began to get into a groove

Then somebody tapped me
"Mansa Musa wants to speak with you"
Walking up to him
He was nodding too
I noticed he had an abundance
So he gave me a couple of jewels
With this insightful information
I could definitely put it to use
Then Nipsey joined in by saying
"Let's all conclude
You don't belong here homie
There's a marathon to continue
Life can be hard
It can appear to be a nightmare
I can sympathize with you
I know life ain't always fair
You special lil' homie
You just have to face those fears
Live out your purpose
You have something to share"

- Heavenly Home

Ghetto Conscious

Chapter 13
Get Out

Ghetto Conscious

When I had awakened
From those dreams
All of a sudden
I had an epiphany
I wanted to get back to playing ball
So I could earn a scholarship
I no longer wanted to understand
The street's wickedness
They'll always be undefeated
The streets will never lose
They don't have love for anyone
Not for me or for you

Loading up semi's
Playing off of emotion
What will it take
To win a championship?
This is thought provoking
Before the guns start smoking
Take a step back
Look around
Have you not noticed
Losing sight of the bigger picture
Can really mess up the focus

- Championship

Two of the greatest philosophers
Known to man
Would have a difficult time
Trying to comprehend
If the fast life is on your mind
Please switch up your plans
Ain't nothing out here worth
Getting caught up in a jam

Plato nor Socrates
Would be able to distinguish
The hard knock philosophy
Extremely difficult
So I narrowed my study
Down to epistemology
My consciousness began to heighten
I relinquished the mental stampede
No longer was I concerned
With understanding the streets
They will always talk...
They will always take...
They love nobody
Yet, we endure the pain
My ideology says
There's more to be gained
You can't enjoy the sunshine
If you don't learn from the rain

- Street Philosophy

The streets will never love you
Nor will they love me
We shouldn't be risking
Our lives or freedom
Just for money...
Respect...
Or for a name...
Some willing to sell their souls
For a bit of street fame
It's cold outside
Hope you know the streets don't play
You get no redos at life
This ain't no arcade

- Heart of the Streets

Gunshots constantly ringing
They stayed shooting outside
I was always told not to go out there
But if I don't go outside
To take my shot
Opportunity
Will think I'm scared...

I have to take my shot!

I can recall being in class
Sharing textbooks with killers
We didn't have enough to go around
There were 40 kids
We only had 17 textbooks
Their biggest fear was to read
So when it was time to partner up
They sat next to me
So what should I be afraid of?

- Take a shot

When I was young
I use to always tell
My daddy I wanted a *BMW*
My daddy would always say
"Son if you ever get that car
It's gone be cause' of you"
Then he would follow up with the question
"Do you know what *BMW* stands for?"
Looking confused I would say "no"
Then his smart answer would be
"Brandon Must Work"
When he said that shit it got on my nerves
I figured all parents bought their kids
cars
Not sure why I was under this impression
Everything my daddy tried to teach me
Later on I would see as valuable lessons
It taught me to have discipline
I developed a great work ethic
It also taught me when you want something
"YOU" have to go get it

-BMW

Psychological warfare
Enabled me
To fight wars mentally
Every thought is calculated
Plans are constructed strategically
The blueprint to success
Is a longevity test
Remember the journey of a million miles
Starts with one step

- One Step at A Time

Ghetto Conscious

Chapter 14
New Day

After all I went through
Allowed me
To no longer be confused
Holding myself accountable
Grabbing the bull by the horns
A hard head made a soft ass
I'm proud to say
I've learned from all the thorns

Way back when
I thought it was all about me
God put me through some things
That were humbling
Life is greater than self
It's not all about me
Had to let the "E" go
So I could really see
I've matured enough
Escaping myself was worth it
Working to live out God's plan
Fulfilling my sole purpose

- Ego

Brandon Vega

As the water evaporates
The mud dries
Returning to dirt
The soil is rich
Although I've been buried
Not sure if I would blossom
But this was a hole
I absolutely could not ditch

Feeling claustrophobic
I can feel myself growing
Stretching in every direction
I'm enjoying the aerobics
Rising above ground
My family depending on my heroics
The things I went through
Forced me to bury my emotions
But if we don't go through anything
How can we keep growing?

- Growth

The tree branch snaps
A loud thud quakes the earth
Seeping into the ground
Returning to dust
From which once came
Waiting for things to come full circle
So that I am born again
What will it be like
Upon the next arrival?
The past life is the future
The process is a cycle
Starting as a pillar
Propped into the ground
Loading in my shell
Ready to burst open
Tucked by my sides
My wings feel paralyzed
Extending my reach
As far as it will go
No longer can I be held
Stretching my spirit
To inhale fresh air

- The Cycle

Ghetto Conscious

From this day forward
My head will be held high
Instead of walking
I'll choose to run
The momentum will allow me
To spread my wings
And fly

Wasn't a big believer in magic
Where I came from
The thought of you
Meticulously developing my life
Never quite dawned
Seeing the work done
Once you waved your wand
God forgive me
For I didn't realize
That I am just one of your pawns
Everything you put me through
Brought maturity and growth
I apologize for my childish ways
As well as my nonchalant approach
The devastation the invasive weeds
inflicted
I couldn't tell I was a rose
Felt I had no value
But I was starkly juxtaposed

- Moving Forward

Walking the straight and narrow
Trying to keep balance
Straddling the line
Takes a ton of talent
Entering the unknown
Stuck in between when the rope snaps
Losing all control
Praying things don't collapse
I've seen people lose
Due to their attitude
Lives were cut short
Prior to reaching maximum altitude
At all times
Purpose must be pursued
We all have choices
Which life will you choose?

- Choices

The ghetto can cut the ambition of one
trying to escape its strong hold. The
reality of the struggle can cause a
resentment, taking up a chunk of the
mind's real estate. Expressing oneself
through sports, art or any other type of
creativity, may be the only time freedom
is felt. The further away from the
light in the tunnel, the more it seems
impossible to ever reach freedom.

As one continues to put one foot in front
of the other, the light that appears at the
end begins to become brighter, indicating
getting closer to understanding. When
one reflects on his or her life, it will
show how connected the past and present
truly is. What the caterpillar perceives
as the end, to the butterfly is just
the beginning. Failure or disappointment
should never be taken personally.

The stigma attached to people that come
from environments like where I'm from,
is a misunderstanding. We are bright, we
have talent, we just need an opportunity.
We need someone that will help cultivate
us into fulfilling our potential. We need
someone to care. I avoided the statistics
that are attached to so many young
black men. I do know I surpassed the age
expectancy, I graduated high school, I
graduated college; which I may add, I am
the first in my family to do so. I also

know that I have never been incarcerated.

But there are questions that often linger in my mind... What if I did not have a father who made sure to discipline me? Or was present in my life? Or a mother that did not love me with all of her heart? What if I never played basketball? Would I have gone to prison? Would I be dead? Where would I be? My friend Rich was my next door neighbor. He was like a big brother to me. He was murdered along with his seven-year-old son. A pure tragedy. His life could have been mine. Things like this give me remorseful feelings. Often times I have flashbacks of our conversations. It saddens me knowing I will never get to speak with him again. He was one person that I knew for sure that wanted to see me succeed.

Moreover, I am thankful for my upbringing; much of what I have been able to accomplish to this point took sacrifice. But luck and chance also has been on my side. Change took effort. I realized that my ignorance was curable. One thing I could afford to change was my way of thinking, way of acting and the way I treated others. The opportunity for me to experience life outside of my neighborhood was beneficial in many ways. Sports played a major role in my life, basketball truly saved my life. It taught me a lot of lessons that I have been able to apply to my life. I have learned discipline, dedication, preparation, teamwork and execution.

Where we come from, is not a choice. Regardless of these things, one must make the best of their circumstances. I have cried, screamed, and have had breakdowns when revisiting my past. But the future springs from the past and the only way to move forward is by acknowledging what got me to this point. It is said, that "art imitates life," well my life was reflected in my art. Writing a book about the story of my life was a surreal process. This was my truth. This was my "Ghetto Conscious."

I can not speak for everyone that grew up in disenfranchised communities, but I am confident that most could probably echo similar sentiments. It is important to me that I give people that have nothing hope, inspiration and motivation. We all have a story. Don't be afraid to share yours. You never know who it might inspire. Remember... anything is possible when you free your mind.

Brandon Vega

Ghetto Conscious

When I began this writing process
the greatest blessing I could have
ever received was born. This poem was
written a few days before you were
born Messiah. I want you to know that
I love you more than anything.

To my Sun,

No matter how exhausting the day is
I'll never let you down
Unconditional love and care
Is what you'll be around
My life revolves around you
I'll always be encouraging
No matter
What path you choose
Your light will illuminate the earth
Keeping the sky employed
The moment we embraced
Emotionally I became overjoyed
Keeping you enlightened
So you are not eclipsed by dark
Teaching you to swim
So you don't learn from sharks
Apologizing now because
I can not save you from everything
Here are a few steps
You must learn as Prince
Before you become King
Have respect for yourself
And for others
Always obey me
As well as your mother

Tell the truth
No matter what
Lies will have you tied up
Being honest is the way you'll develop trust
Never dwell in the past
Be able to forgive yourself
You'll learn money is not everything
Health and knowledge is true wealth
Get your shine on
Dim your lights for no one
Sun block out distractions
Don't let them cloud your judgment
Most important of them all
Never be afraid to
Have a relationship with God
Sun God is amazing
Follow the trail
He is blazing
When things seem wrong
Trust and believe
There is no mistaking
The key to life
Will simply be patience

Sun rise to the summit of the mountain
There will be valleys and peaks
You can travel much further
And accomplish way more than you think

Love always,
Your daddy

If you made it to this point of the book, thank you for reading.

Acknowledgements

I am forever indebted to Sandra Powell, Tikia Douglas, Michel-Ange Chevry, Joann Jones and Vivi Smith for their keen insight, editing and ongoing support throughout this project. You ladies did a wonderful job helping me focus during this process. Also, I would like to thank all of the early draft readers for taking the time to read and give me feedback.

A special thanks to Gladwin Denbow. You have always believed in me, you have always been willing to extend a helping hand. Much love goes to my mentor, Kenny Brown, who saw a kid at the age of nineteen that was hungry to learn, eager to grow and anxious to succeed. You never doubted me, you have always inspired, encouraged and motivated me. Thank you.

To Mike Ostlund and Jake Atwood, thank you guys for giving me an opportunity to play college basketball. Forever Snow. To Pat Kelsey, thank you for believing in me through the good and bad. I am forever grateful. To Jarrod Calhoun, thank you for giving me an opportunity to finish what I started. Thank you for believing in EATN and what it represents. To Joe Mazzulla, who would ask me everyday during my senior year "what is your purpose?" in which I would respond, "I didn't know." Thank you for being extremely hard on me and showing me tough love. I think I have found it. Joe you have my deepest gratitude.

To my former college professor Adolphus Belk, Jr., my friend Greg Hinton and my former high school teacher Ashley Toussaint; thank you all for showing me that as a black man, it is okay to be intellectual and articulate, while remaining true to self. I needed that. To Todd Van Brocklin, Rob Neilson and Robert Cable, you guys have been father figures to me. You guys never saw my age or race; you only saw someone that possessed a gift. Everyone has talent, but only believers have gifts. You all helped me believe. I can not thank you enough. To Mr. Charles my first basketball coach, thank you for your selflessness and most importantly, thank you for leading with your actions.

I want to thank my family for all of the valuable lessons and support throughout my journey. To my dad, it is simple as this... "I understand

now." And I'm grateful for the way
you raised me. I love you. Thank you.
To my mama, your love has made up for
the times of your absence. I love you.
To both of my step parents Valerie
Adams and Antron Frazier, you both
gave me something different, I thank
you both for all you have done for me.
To my granddad LeRoy Rainey, thank you
for your selfless acts of kindness. I
definitely have that Rainey blood in
me. To my grandma Deloris, I love you.
To my cousin Eno Valiente and Maria
Lawrence, thank you for raising me in a
house full of kids and treating me like
your own. I want to thank my Godparents
Marvin and Pam English for all of their
love.

To my cousin's Ena, Rondre, Tara, Tera,
Xavier, Jeff, Andrea, Lisa, Raychelle,
Tony, Antwan, Ray-Ray, Nick, Tevin,
Jr., Raymond, and Josh – you all have
helped me in ways you'll never know.
I thank you all and I love each and
every one of you. To my sister Armaria
I love you more than life itself and
I hope I have set a good example as a
big brother. To my sister Valencia,
I love you and appreciate you. To my
late, great Uncle Dale aka "Big Smoove"
the words of encouragement you always
shared will stay with me forever. Thank
you for being a great example of hard-
work. To my brother Deandre, this is

what life after basketball looks like.
I hope I have set the bar high and have
inspired you to do big things. "We only
know one way!"

 To all the guys I grew up around or
under; "Pootie," Marquise, Jarrod,
"Tuck," "Popey", "Mikey," "Tay-Tay,"
Kenny, Keith, "Quez," "Piff" "J.J.,"
"Pooky," "Facts," "Strokes," "Worm,"
"Poppy," "Tray," "White Boy," "Mikey,"
"Monk," "Lil B," Tyrone, David,
Quinton, Tony, Marlon, Chester, "Zay,"
Carlton, Greg, "Bernie Mac," "B.C.,"
"Ears," "Butchy," Bobby, "Reef,"
Outten, Christian, "Man-Man", Chaz,
"Slay," "Reese," Isaac, Cleveland,
Laroy, "Lil J," Dalvin, "Ton,"
Herschel, Lester and Terrell. A special
shout out to you all. Without y'all, I
would not have turned out to be the man
that I am today. There are so many more
people to name, please know that you
all are greatly appreciated!

And last but not least, to the only
place I could have been from... Carol
City. You made me, you molded me, you
raised me. In a place where statistics
were unfavorable, I survived. You are
the reason why I have the confidence
to go anywhere and be successful. You
prepared me to be mentally tough. Now
I understand why God placed me in your
jungle. Thank you Lord.